WILLIAM WALTON

TWO PIECES FOR SOLO CELLO

EDITED BY
HUGH MACDONALD

MUSIC DEPARTMENT
OXFORD
UNIVERSITY PRESS

OXFORD
UNIVERSITY PRESS

Great Clarendon Street, Oxford OX2 6DP, England
198 Madison Avenue, New York, NY 10016, USA

Oxford University Press is a department of the University of Oxford.
It furthers the University's aim of excellence in research, scholarship,
and education by publishing worldwide in

Oxford New York
Auckland Cape Town Hong Kong Karachi
Kuala Lumpur Madrid Melbourne Mexico City Nairobi
New Delhi Shanghai Taipei Toronto

With offices in

Argentina Austria Brazil Chile Czech Republic France Greece
Guatemala Hungary Italy Japan Poland Portugal Singapore
South Korea Switzerland Thailand Turkey Ukraine Vietnam

This edition published 2009

ISBN 978–0–19–336620–6

Music origination by Enigma Music Production Services, Amersham, Bucks.
Printed in Great Britain on acid-free paper by
Caligraving Ltd., Thetford, Norfolk

Tema (per Variazioni) per Cello Solo

(from Music for a Prince)

WILLIAM WALTON

Printed in Great Britain

OXFORD UNIVERSITY PRESS, MUSIC DEPARTMENT, GREAT CLARENDON STREET, OXFORD OX2 6DP *for Mstislav Rostropovich*

Passacaglia
for Violoncello Solo

Edited by Mstislav Rostropovich

WILLIAM WALTON

Lento espressivo ♩ = *c.*60

marc.
marc.
poco rit. - - - a tempo
poco rit.
a tempo
rit. - - - - - - - a tempo
rit. - - a tempo

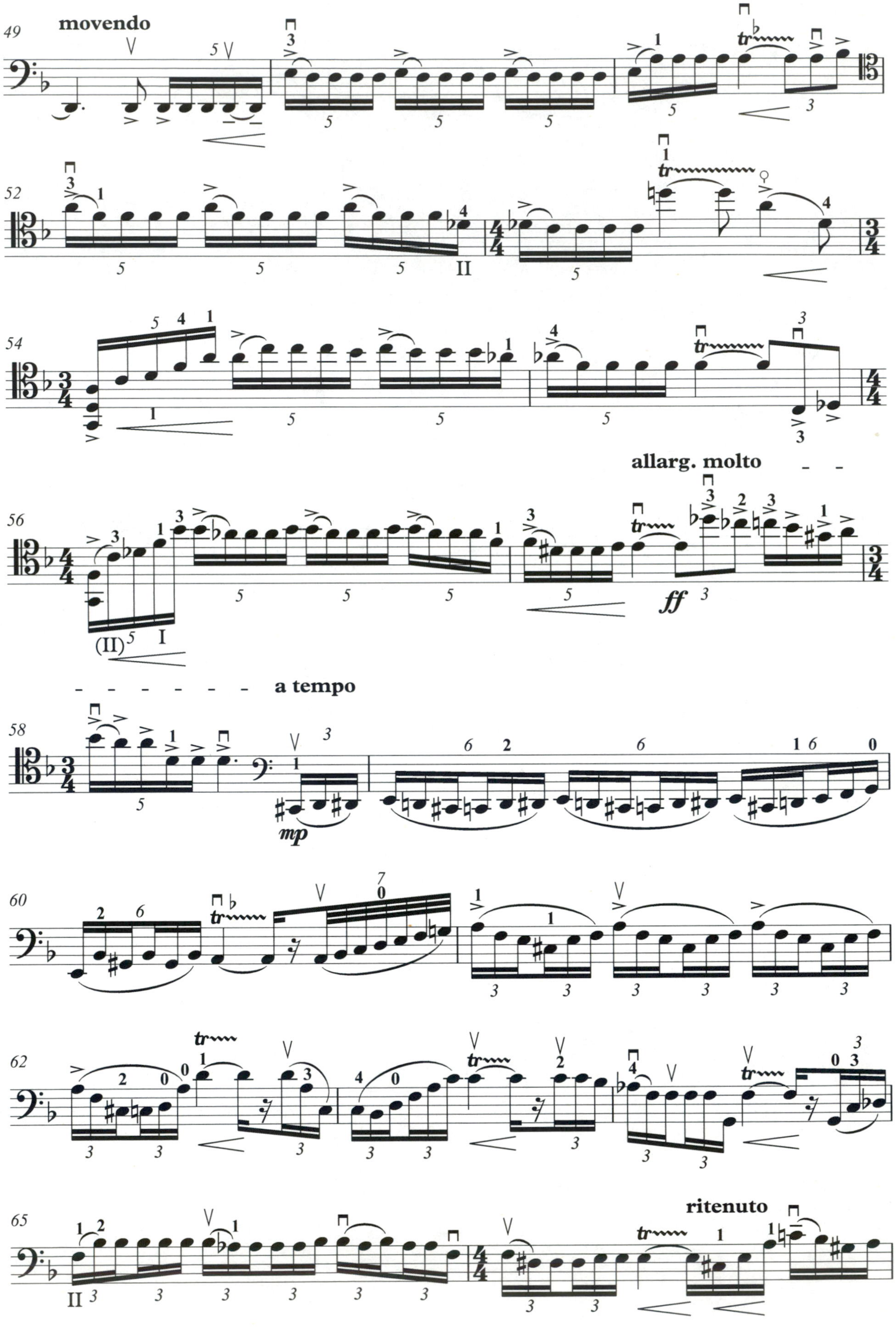
movendo
allarg. molto
ff
a tempo
mp
ritenuto

a tempo
poco
allarg.
♩ = c.56
arco
pizz.
mf
tranquillo espressivo
arco
p
dim.
Subito vivace ♩. = c.112
pp spiccato
p
ff
mp
ff
mp
ff
mp

mp cresc.
p cresc.
ff strepitoso
pizz.

(Early Elementary)

Hymn Primer

A Very Easy Book of Hymns
For Piano or Electronic Keyboard

By Wesley Schaum

Foreword

This book is designed to make familiar hymns as easy as possible. A student with just six to eight weeks study will be able to start enjoying this album.

The pieces are arranged in five-finger position with melody divided between the hands. A minimum of finger numbers is used. Large, widely spaced notes help make music reading easier. Rests have been purposely omitted so the student can focus on the notes.

Duet accompaniments offer many possibilities for recitals and Sunday school participation. The duets help provide rhythmic training and ensemble experience especially valuable to beginners. The person playing the accompaniment is free to add pedal according to his/her own taste.

The duets are recommended for use at home as well as at the lesson. However, the student should work alone at first until the notes and rhythm of the solo part are secure.

Index

Schaum Publications, Inc.

Exclusively Distributed By
HAL•LEONARD® CORPORATION
7777 W. Bluemound Rd. P.O. Box 13819 Milwaukee, WI 53213

ISBN-13: 978-1-936098-63-7

09-30

Faith of Our Fathers

Moderato
3
f
Faith of our fa - thers liv - ing still
1

5
In spite of dun - geon, fire___ and sword,

Duet Accompaniment (Stem up = R.H. Stem down = L.H.)

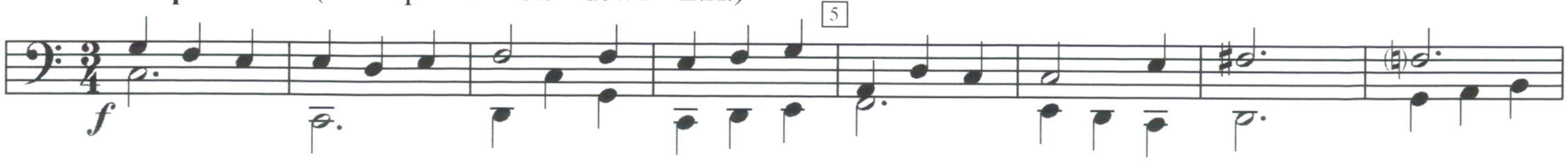
f
5

9
O how our hearts beat high with joy
13
When - e'er we hear that glo - rious word.
17
Faith of our fa - thers, ho - ly faith!
21
We will be true to Thee till death.

Duet Accompaniment (continued)

9
13
17
21

Jesus Loves Me This I Know

Semplice
mp
Je - sus loves me, this I know, For the Bi - ble tells me so.
5
Lit - tle ones to Him be - long. They are weak but He is strong.
9
Yes, Je - sus loves me, Yes, Je - sus loves me,
13
Yes, Je - sus loves me, The Bi - ble tells me so.

Duet Accompaniment

mp
5
9
13

Fairest Lord Jesus

Andante
mf
Fair - est Lord Je - sus, Rul - er of all
na - ture, O Thou of God and man the
Son, Thee will I cher - ish, Thee will I
hon - or, Thou, my soul's glo - ry, joy and crown.

Duet Accompaniment

mf

Holy, Holy, Holy!

Tell Me the Stories of Jesus

Dolce
mp
Tell me the sto - ries of Je - sus I
love to hear; Things I would ask Him to
6
Duet Accompaniment
mp
6

11
tell me If He were here.
16
Scenes by the way - side,
21
3 5 2
Tales of the sea, Sto - ries of
27
Je - sus, Tell them to me.

Duet Accompaniment (continued)

11
16
21
27

Now Thank We All Our God

Duet Accompaniment

O Worship the King

Praise to the Lord the Almighty

Giocoso
4
f
Praise to the Lord, the Al - might - y, the
2

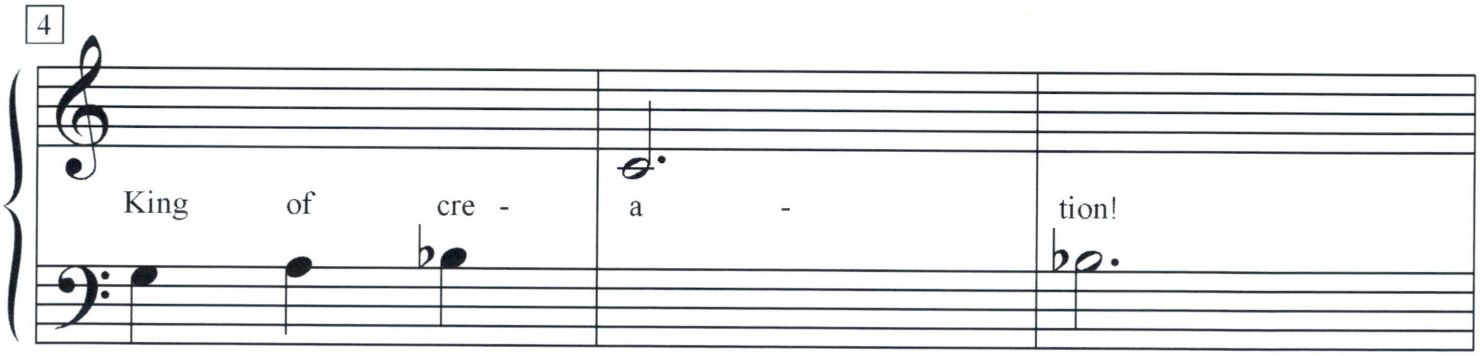
4
King of cre - a - tion!

Duet Accompaniment

4
f

Teacher's Note: If the pupil is in the early grades in school and has not yet had fractions, do not attempt to explain the dotted quarter note-eighth note rhythm. The rule to follow is this: *experience should precede explanation.* Teach the rhythm by rote. Delay the explanation until the situation arises at a later time when the student has acquired fraction readiness.

Duet Accompaniment (continued)

As With Gladness Men of Old

Duet Accompaniment

A Mighty Fortress Is Our God

Duet Accompaniment

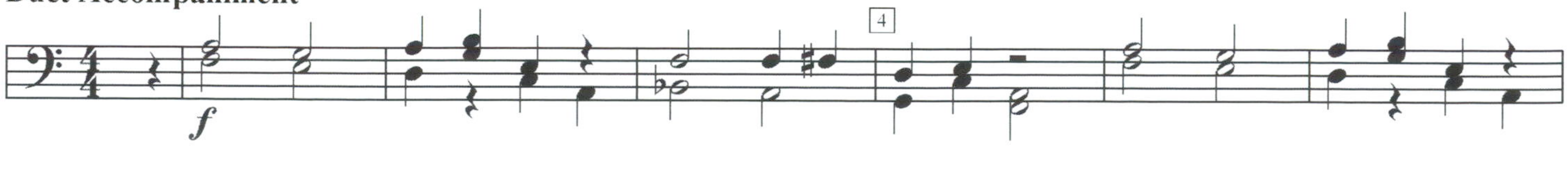

mp
p
mf
mp
mp
p
pp

HAL•LEONARD INSTRUMENTAL PLAY-ALONG

Your favorite songs are arranged just for solo instrumentalists with this outstanding series. Each book includes great full-accompaniment play-along audio so you can sound just like a pro!

Check out **halleonard.com** for songlists and more titles!

12 Pop Hits
12 songs

00261790 Flute	00261795 Horn
00261791 Clarinet	00261796 Trombone
00261792 Alto Sax	00261797 Violin
00261793 Tenor Sax	00261798 Viola
00261794 Trumpet	00261799 Cello

The Very Best of Bach
15 selections

00225371 Flute	00225376 Horn
00225372 Clarinet	00225377 Trombone
00225373 Alto Sax	00225378 Violin
00225374 Tenor Sax	00225379 Viola
00225375 Trumpet	00225380 Cello

The Beatles
15 songs

00225330 Flute	00225335 Horn
00225331 Clarinet	00225336 Trombone
00225332 Alto Sax	00225337 Violin
00225333 Tenor Sax	00225338 Viola
00225334 Trumpet	00225339 Cello

Chart Hits
12 songs

00146207 Flute	00146212 Horn
00146208 Clarinet	00146213 Trombone
00146209 Alto Sax	00146214 Violin
00146210 Tenor Sax	00146211 Trumpet
00146216 Cello	

Christmas Songs
12 songs

00146855 Flute	00146863 Horn
00146858 Clarinet	00146864 Trombone
00146859 Alto Sax	00146866 Violin
00146860 Tenor Sax	00146867 Viola
00146862 Trumpet	00146868 Cello

Contemporary Broadway
15 songs

00298704 Flute	00298709 Horn
00298705 Clarinet	00298710 Trombone
00298706 Alto Sax	00298711 Violin
00298707 Tenor Sax	00298712 Viola
00298708 Trumpet	00298713 Cello

Disney Movie Hits
12 songs

00841420 Flute	00841424 Horn
00841687 Oboe	00841425 Trombone
00841421 Clarinet	00841426 Violin
00841422 Alto Sax	00841427 Viola
00841686 Tenor Sax	00841428 Cello
00841423 Trumpet	

Prices, contents, and availability subject to change without notice.

Disney Solos
12 songs

00841404 Flute	00841506 Oboe
00841406 Alto Sax	00841409 Trumpet
00841407 Horn	00841410 Violin
00841411 Viola	00841412 Cello
00841405 Clarinet/Tenor Sax	
00841408 Trombone/Baritone	
00841553 Mallet Percussion	

Dixieland Favorites
15 songs

00268756 Flute	0068759 Trumpet
00268757 Clarinet	00268760 Trombone
00268758 Alto Sax	

Billie Eilish
9 songs

00345648 Flute	00345653 Horn
00345649 Clarinet	00345654 Trombone
00345650 Alto Sax	00345655 Violin
00345651 Tenor Sax	00345656 Viola
00345652 Trumpet	00345657 Cello

Favorite Movie Themes
13 songs

00841166 Flute	00841168 Trumpet
00841167 Clarinet	00841170 Trombone
00841169 Alto Sax	00841296 Violin

Gospel Hymns
15 songs

00194648 Flute	00194654 Trombone
00194649 Clarinet	00194655 Violin
00194650 Alto Sax	00194656 Viola
00194651 Tenor Sax	00194657 Cello
00194652 Trumpet	

Great Classical Themes
15 songs

00292727 Flute	00292733 Horn
00292728 Clarinet	00292735 Trombone
00292729 Alto Sax	00292736 Violin
00292730 Tenor Sax	00292737 Viola
00292732 Trumpet	00292738 Cello

The Greatest Showman
8 songs

00277389 Flute	00277394 Horn
00277390 Clarinet	00277395 Trombone
00277391 Alto Sax	00277396 Violin
00277392 Tenor Sax	00277397 Viola
00277393 Trumpet	00277398 Cello

Irish Favorites
31 songs

00842489 Flute	00842495 Trombone
00842490 Clarinet	00842496 Violin
00842491 Alto Sax	00842497 Viola
00842493 Trumpet	00842498 Cello
00842494 Horn	

Michael Jackson
11 songs

00119495 Flute	00119499 Trumpet
00119496 Clarinet	00119501 Trombone
00119497 Alto Sax	00119503 Violin
00119498 Tenor Sax	00119502 Accomp.

Jazz & Blues
14 songs

00841438 Flute	00841441 Trumpet
00841439 Clarinet	00841443 Trombone
00841440 Alto Sax	00841444 Violin
00841442 Tenor Sax	

Jazz Classics
12 songs

00151812 Flute	00151816 Trumpet
00151813 Clarinet	00151818 Trombone
00151814 Alto Sax	00151819 Violin
00151815 Tenor Sax	00151821 Cello

Les Misérables
13 songs

00842292 Flute	00842297 Horn
00842293 Clarinet	00842298 Trombone
00842294 Alto Sax	00842299 Violin
00842295 Tenor Sax	00842300 Viola
00842296 Trumpet	00842301 Cello

Metallica
12 songs

02501327 Flute	02502454 Horn
02501339 Clarinet	02501329 Trombone
02501332 Alto Sax	02501334 Violin
02501333 Tenor Sax	02501335 Viola
02501330 Trumpet	02501338 Cello

Motown Classics
15 songs

00842572 Flute	00842576 Trumpet
00842573 Clarinet	00842578 Trombone
00842574 Alto Sax	00842579 Violin
00842575 Tenor Sax	

Pirates of the Caribbean
16 songs

00842183 Flute	00842188 Horn
00842184 Clarinet	00842189 Trombone
00842185 Alto Sax	00842190 Violin
00842186 Tenor Sax	00842191 Viola
00842187 Trumpet	00842192 Cello

Queen
17 songs

00285402 Flute	00285407 Horn
00285403 Clarinet	00285408 Trombone
00285404 Alto Sax	00285409 Violin
00285405 Tenor Sax	00285410 Viola
00285406 Trumpet	00285411 Cello

Simple Songs
14 songs

00249081 Flute	00249087 Horn
00249093 Oboe	00249089 Trombone
00249082 Clarinet	00249090 Violin
00249083 Alto Sax	00249091 Viola
00249084 Tenor Sax	00249092 Cello
00249086 Trumpet	00249094 Mallets

Superhero Themes
14 songs

00363195 Flute	00363200 Horn
00363196 Clarinet	00363201 Trombone
00363197 Alto Sax	00363202 Violin
00363198 Tenor Sax	00363203 Viola
00363199 Trumpet	00363204 Cello

Star Wars
16 songs

00350900 Flute	00350907 Horn
00350913 Oboe	00350908 Trombone
00350903 Clarinet	00350909 Violin
00350904 Alto Sax	00350910 Viola
00350905 Tenor Sax	00350911 Cello
00350906 Trumpet	00350914 Mallet

Taylor Swift
15 songs

00842532 Flute	00842537 Horn
00842533 Clarinet	00842538 Trombone
00842534 Alto Sax	00842539 Violin
00842535 Tenor Sax	00842540 Viola
00842536 Trumpet	00842541 Cello

Video Game Music
13 songs

00283877 Flute	00283883 Horn
00283878 Clarinet	00283884 Trombone
00283879 Alto Sax	00283885 Violin
00283880 Tenor Sax	00283886 Viola
00283882 Trumpet	00283887 Cello

Wicked
13 songs

00842236 Flute	00842241 Horn
00842237 Clarinet	00842242 Trombone
00842238 Alto Sax	00842243 Violin
00842239 Tenor Sax	00842244 Viola
00842240 Trumpet	00842245 Cello

HAL•LEONARD®